Kvetch as
Kvetch Can

Kvetch as Kvetch Can

JEWISH CARTOONS

Ken Krimstein

Clarkson Potter/Publishers
New York

For Alex, Noah, Milo & Ruby

www.crownpublishing.com
www.clarksonpotter.com

CLARKSON POTTER is a trademark and POTTER
with colophon is a registered trademark of
Random House, Inc.

Library of Congress Cataloging-in-Publication Data
Krimstein, Ken.
    Kvetch as Kvetch Can / Ken Krimstein — 1st Ed.
1. Jews—Caricatures and Cartoons. 2. Jewish wit and
Humor, Pictorial. I. Title
NC1763.J4K75 2010   2009051485
741.5'6973—dc 22

ISBN 978-0-307-58888-3

Printed in the United States of America

Design by Jane Treuhaft

10 9 8 7 6 5 4 3 2 1

First Edition

The Whole Megillah!

Introduction

In many ways, Jews are the perfect topic for a book of cartoons. (Then again, so is bodybuilding, but, alas, I am woefully ill-equipped to tackle that subject, so Jews are what you get.) At first I thought, How do I throw a net around five thousand years or so of kvetching? Thankfully, a handful of key themes poked right up:

First, of course, FOOD. Eating. The true topic A. I was going to start with breakfast, but generally, the main topic of conversation at breakfast is what's for

HALF SOUR

lunch, and at lunch, we're mostly talking about dinner, so it wasn't easy to curb my appetite for this subject.

After food, there's the subject of IDENTITY. Or, to put it another way, when is a Jewfro not a Jewfro?

Following close on its heels (Prada) is FAMILY. Not surprisingly, one of the "tribe" made quite a name for himself mining this topic. But, with all due respect to Dr. Freud, when it comes to family, for Jews, it's way more than whether or not to sit Aunt Sylvia next to Cousin Harold at Josh's Bar Mitzvah. Or is it? Yes, blood is thicker than borscht.

SALE!
MORE!
1/2
OFF!

What is a religion without HOLIDAYS? And what kind of religion calls an entire day sitting in a suit in a stuffy room full of starving people who are biblically prohibited from brushing their teeth a holiday? (A: The Jewish kind, that's what.)

On the topic of LEARNING AND CULTURE, Jews are a natural. Scientists. Orchestra conductors. People who make sitcoms exploring the eschatological* significance of babka. (Oh, there I go thinking of food again.)

* Look it up, Mr. Einstein!

And, finally, the Big Kahuna, the greatest contribution of the Jewish people to the history of the world, not counting the lox, eggs, and onions at Barney Greengrass.

Before the Jews, people used to get stuff done by bashing their neighbors over the head with the thighbone of a yak.

Once the Jews hit the scene, a far more lethal, subtle, dare I say delicious form of behavior modification took control—the silent sledgehammer, the neutron bomb of child-rearing, GUILT.

Well, that's about it. I'm getting hungry—and I've got to get back to my bench presses. Enjoy.

"Just a SLIVER..."

(Food)

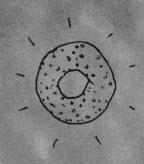

CHAIM RABINOWITZ
FEEDS HIS
GEFILTE FISH

The First Kreplach

14

Ice Cream Cohen

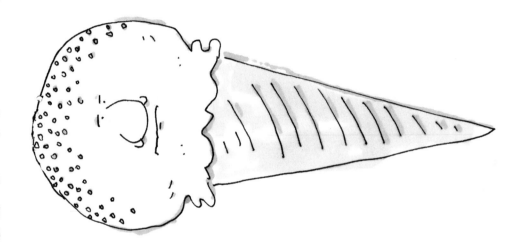

Jewish Deli Coffee

WE'ARE ANNOYED TO SERVE YOU

Rabinically Approved Celebrity Deli Sandwiches

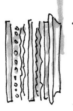

The "Jackie Mason"

The "Sandy Koufax"

The "Philip Roth"

The "Alan Dershowitz"

"THE MATZO BALLS CAME OUT A LITTLE HEAVY."

Christmas in China

"喂，我們叫些猶太外賣吧！"*

"喂，我們叫些猶太外賣吧！"*

"喂，我們叫些猶太外賣吧！"*

"喂，我們叫些猶太外賣吧！"*

"喂，我們叫些猶太外賣吧！"*

"喂，我們叫些猶太外賣吧！"*

*"Let's order Jewish"

"Funny... you don't look ________"

(Identity, please)

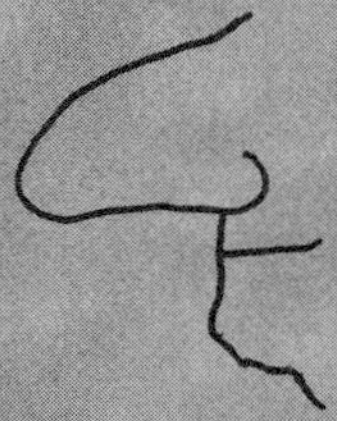

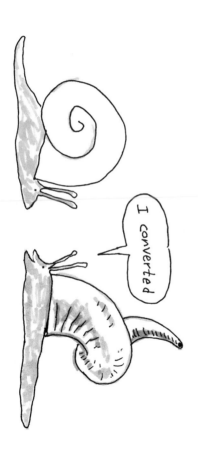

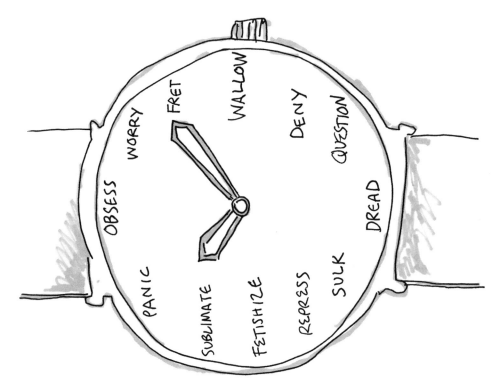

For The Graduate

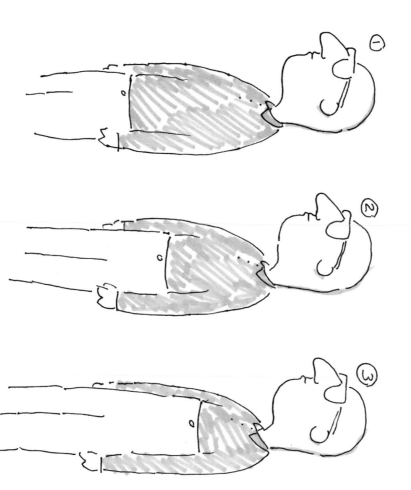

HOW JEWISH MEN AGE

Jewish
MADE

1. If Person you meet has been to Camp Ramah — YES → | NO | STOP

2. If Person has a sister who

4. If at Wharton the person went to their BBYO reunion and met no less than 5 people with parents in Boca, Boynton, or Delray — YES ↑ | NO | STOP

SHINS

6. If person hails from Scarsdale, Shaker Heights,

7. If person has donated more than $500 to UJA — $ — Y↑ N↓

8. If Person has charge account at Barneys, Bloomies, and Bendel's

Geography
SIMPLE

graduated from Brandeis↴

③ If Person who graduated
from Brandeis went on to Wharton

→ YES → NO → STOP

⑤ If person subscribes to HEEB and JEWCY
or has all of Matisyahu's CDs/MP3s

→ YES → NO → STOP

Highland Park or Brentwood

↑ YES → NO → STOP!!!

NO ← YES

⑨ If Person Tivos Larry David,
Jon Stewart { IF NOT → STOP

YES

graduated from Brandeis↴ NO → STOP

YES

NO → STOP

IT IS YOU!

31

How Jewish Are You?

Choose the face that best describes how you feel <u>all the time</u>.

0 — A-OK!

2 — COULD BE WORSE.

4 — LIFE'S A PICNIC.

6 — WHAT DO I LOOK LIKE? A CLOWN? I'LL GET BY...

8 — OY, WHAT IF I WAS TO TELL YOU, WOULD IT MAKE ANY KIND OF DIFFERENCE?

10 — I'M FINE, I'M FINE...

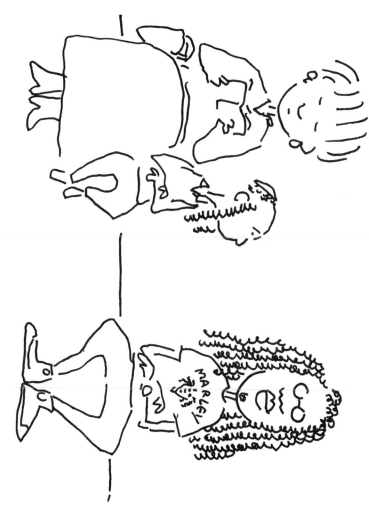

Beth Shalom

Beth Teitelbaum

Beth El

Beth Torah

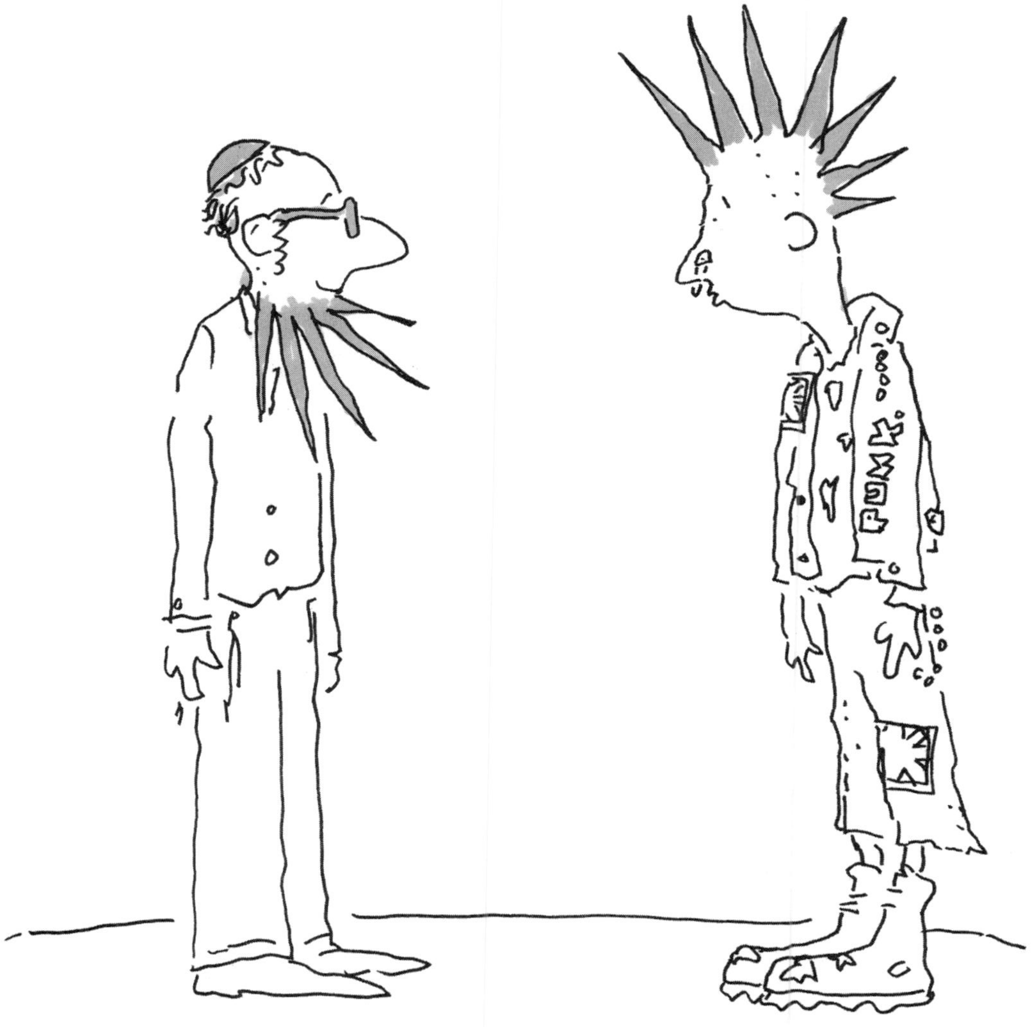
PUNK

A big wind blows
through Crown Heights

36

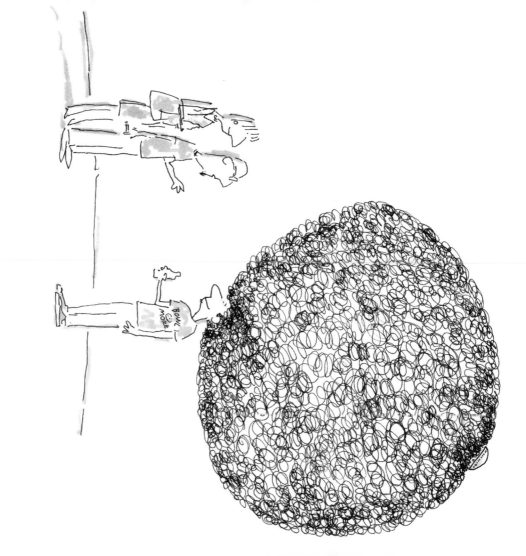

"LOVE YOUR YARMULKE!"

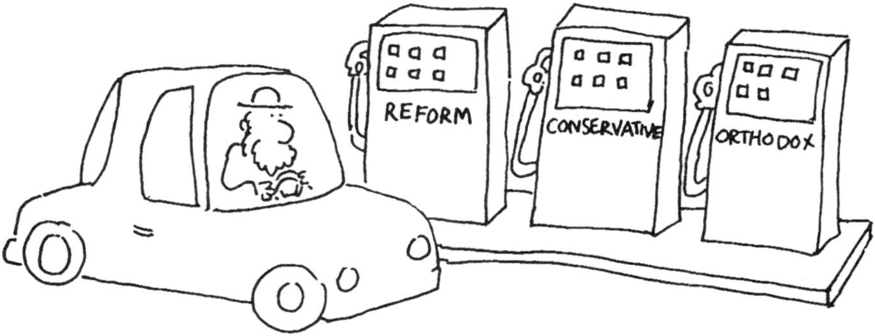
REFORM
CONSERVATIVE
ORTHODOX

"HE'S A JEW — BUT HE'S A BACON-EATING, WINDSURFING, SATURDAY-WORKING, TOOLBOX-OWNING, CHURCH-GOING KIND OF JEW."

"YOU'RE JEWISH."

From
Mishpochah
to
Machatunim

(All in the family)

"CONGRATULATIONS, IT'S A CORPORATE LITIGATION ATTORNEY AT A VERY NICE FIRM."

"MAZEL-TOV"

44

"We named him after his great-great-grandfather."

SKATE SHOP

"I'D LIKE A HELMET FOR HIS HELMET."

"LOOK, MOM AND DAD, IT'S A CLASSIC 7 WITH OUTDOOR SPACE, RIVER VIEWS, LOW MAINTENANCE, PARKING, AND A GRANDFATHERED-IN J-51 TAX ABATEMENT."

47

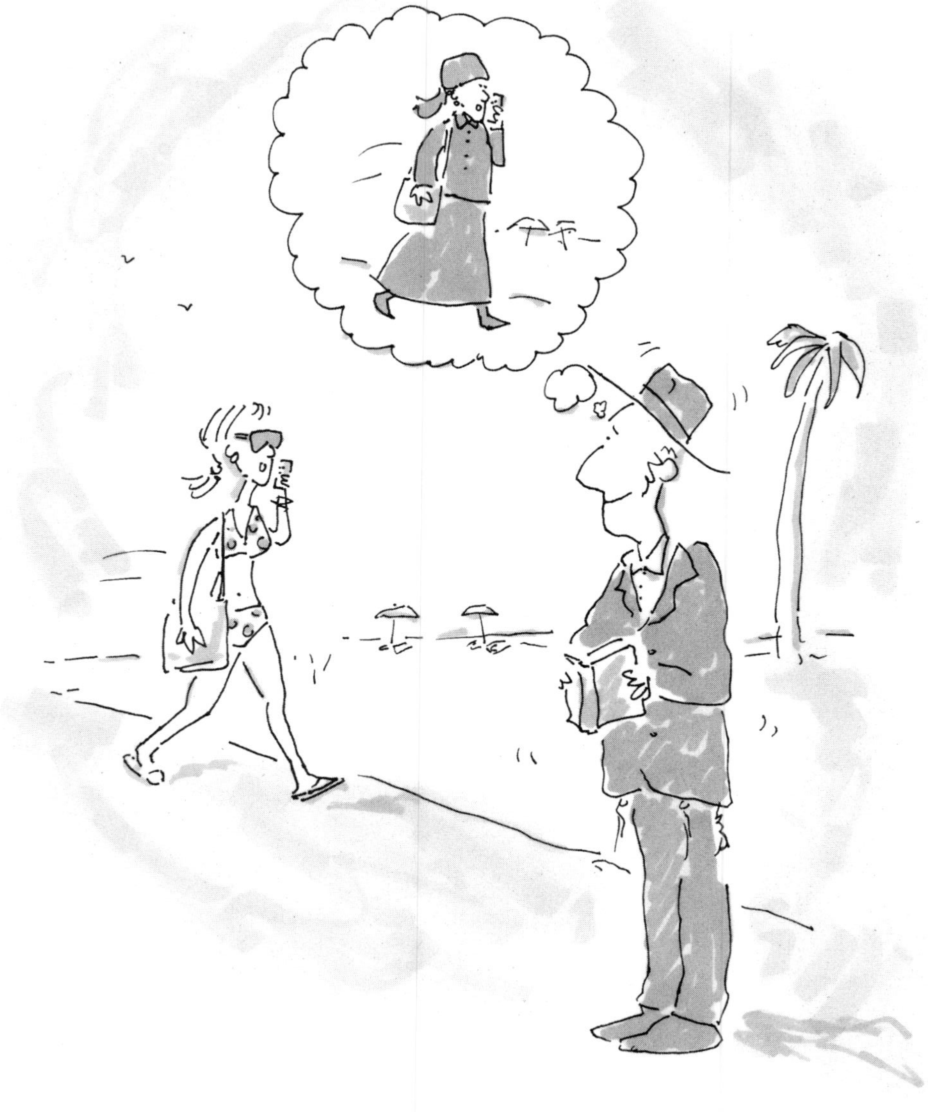

"NOT TONIGHT, DAVID, HONEY, I'M HAVING BRAIN SURGERY."

"LET'S PRETEND I'M A SIX-FOOT-SEVEN
ISRAELI CARDIOLOGIST WITH A
DEGREE FROM PRINCETON AND A
FAMILY VACATION HOUSE IN
ST. BARTS."

R. I. P.
MORRIS GOLDSTEIN
LOVING HUSBAND, FATHER, GRANDFATHER
R. I. P.
JANICE GOLDSTEIN
MORRIE, WHY'D YOU HAVE TO PICK SUCH A DRAFTY SPOT??!!!

Hannukah ?.
Hanuka ?.
Chanukah ?.

(Life's a holiday)

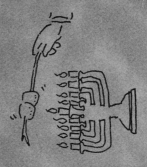

For the sin we have committed by willfully consuming a double whopper with cheese while listening to Blue Öyster Cult in a nonironic fashion.

·B'NAI ZION·
HIGH HOLIDAY TICKET HOLDERS
EXPRESS: TEN SINS OR LESS ONLY LANE

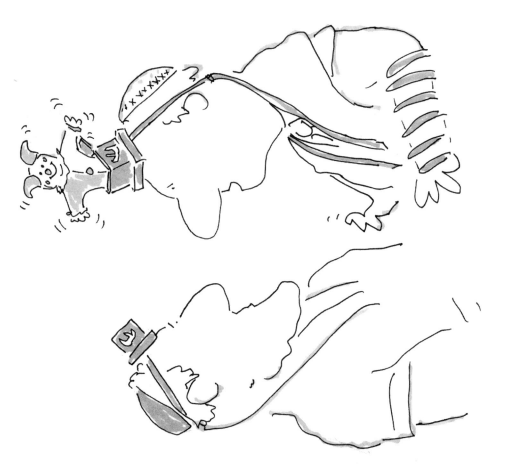

BILLY THE KIDDUSH

"HE CELEBRATES BOTH."

NORTH POLE

60

"WE'RE NOT CALLING IT A CHRISTMAS TREE OR A HANUKKAH BUSH — WE'RE CALLING IT A 'DECEMBER HOLIDAY GREEN THING THAT DIES.'"

Last time I was at synagogue

Roman Empire Falls

Columbus Discovers America

Man walks on the Moon

BANNED BAR MITZVAH

"The Funky Babka"

"The Meshugah Audit"

"The Insider Trader"

Why is this Knight different?

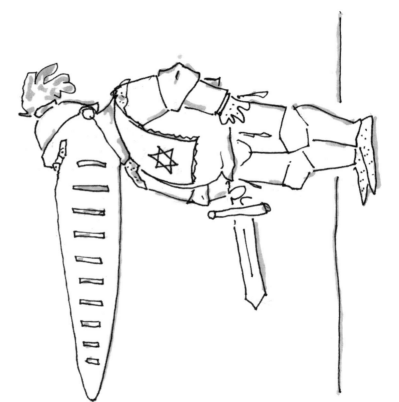

Helen Keller, at her first Seder, accidentally reads a Matzo.

Updated Seder Plate

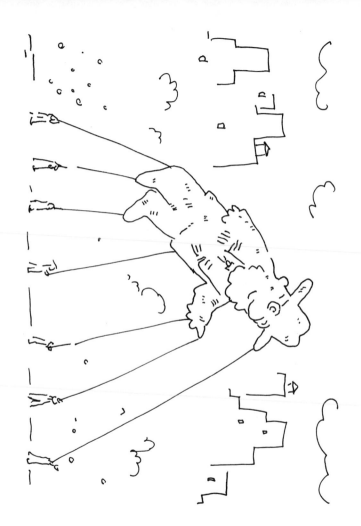

At The Macy's Passover Day Parade

69

Culture Shmulture

(learning shmurning)

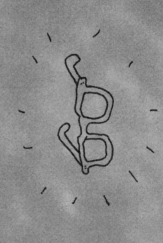

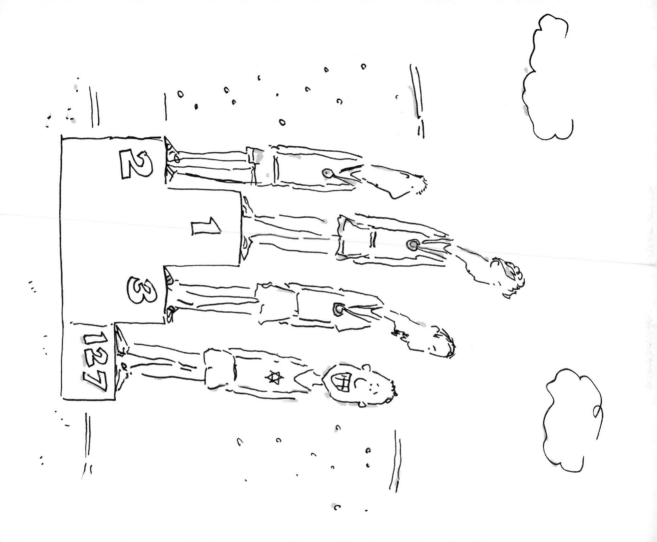

Can I call you back? I'm out walking the rabbis.

At Jewish Summer Camp

Today we're going to learn how to weave a lawsuit out of lanyard.

74

"THERE ARE SEVERAL PEOPLE I'D LIKE TO THANK, AND EVEN MORE I'D LIKE TO SHTUP."

"I LOVE YOUR ANALYSIS OF THE TELEOLOGICAL DYNAMISM IN SPINOZA'S HERMENEUTICS — BUT COULD YOU MAYBE WORK IN SOME TEENAGE JEWISH VAMPIRES?"

At Bubbe's Condo
You paid WHAT for that?
You paid WHAT for that?
You paid WHAT for that?

OYKEA ®

BUBBNG NAGG

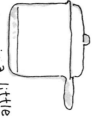

- Ugly sofa that turns into a comfy bed for Bubbe to encamp for a night – or a nightmare.
- See companion piece— ZADDNG NAGG.

FRESPN

- Throw in a little of this, a little of that.
- Oh, it was nothing...
- Daughter-in-law safe.

DRK SHLPR

- Heavy-duty bag designed to carry all manner of stuff.
- Guaranteed that you won't be able to find anything you are looking for in it.

ANGR

- Wall Lamp that could, in theory, project bright light but won't because how the Hell are you supposed to be able to follow the damn instructions and put it _in the_ Wall!!!

The Secret History

JOHN   PAUL   GEORGE   RINGO   MENDEL

The Pillsbury Golem

"YES, BUT HAVE YOU GUYS TRIED THE PASTRAMI AT ZINGERMAN'S?"

82

BOB DYLAN: THE ZOROASTRIAN PHASE*

* Born Robert Zimmerman

"That's OK, I'll sit in the DARK."

(Guilt and other delights)

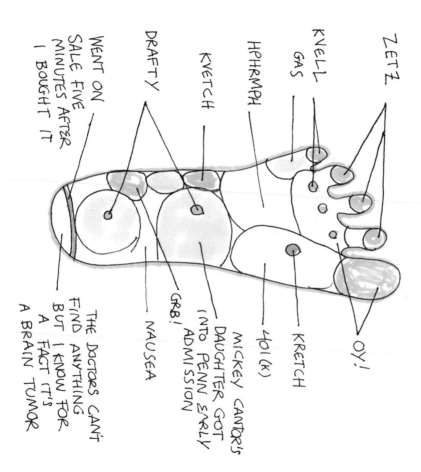

Jewish Reflexology

ZETZ

KVELL
GAS

HPHRMPH

KVETCH

DRAFTY

WENT ON
SALE FIVE
MINUTES AFTER
I BOUGHT IT

OY!

KRETCH

401 (K)

MICKEY CANTOR'S
DAUGHTER GOT
INTO PENN EARLY
ADMISSION

GRB!

NAUSEA

THE DOCTORS CAN'T
FIND ANYTHING
BUT I KNOW FOR
A FACT IT'S
A BRAIN TUMOR

FOGELSON, GRINBERG, SCHWARTZ, LEFKOWITZ, SILVERSTEIN, LEVIN & MURPHY
Murphy's the plumber.

Goys Я US

FORMERLY "THE ATHLETIC CLUB"
(still restricted)

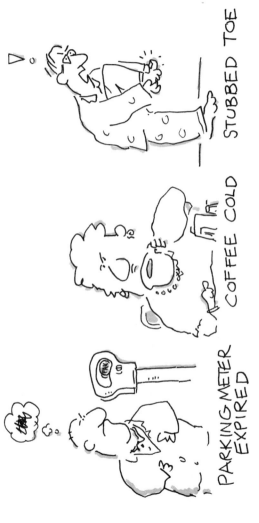

CONDOLENCE CARDS
DEATH BY STONING
DEATH BY BURNING
IMPALED
SEVENFOLD VENGEANCE
FIRST BORN
DEATH BY DROWNING

acknowledgments

Thank you: Sam Gross; Bruce Jay Friedman; A. J. Jacobs; Cindy Kaplan; the late (great) Jay Kennedy; Dusty Wright; Ross Abrash; Jason Roeder; Jim Stallard; Jennifer Lyons, my agent; Aliza Fogelson, my editor; Jane Treuhaft, my art director; Peggy Paul, factotum; Mags Sinclair, who ordered my wife to take my cartoons to Punch; Lorna Sinclair; Jordie Krimstein, who stocked our home with markers cadged from the ad agency; Joan Krimstein; Al Spriester, my high school band director; Hyman Krimstein, my great-grandfather, who got on a boat in 1899; and Moses, without whom...

SEE, I WASN'T JUST KVETCHING!